Maths in Stories

Acknowledgements

Our thanks to children and teachers at the following schools:

Baring Primary School and Nursery, Lewisham
Forster Park Primary School, Lewisham
Ridgeway Primary School, Croydon
St George the Martyr CofE Primary School, Camden

Thanks to all of the Foundation Stage practitioners in Lewisham and around the country who have shared their experiences, views and enthusiasm.

Thanks also to the children from schools and settings in Lewisham whose fantastic drawings are celebrated throughout this book.

Published by BEAM Education
Maze Workshops
72a Southgate Road
London N1 3JT
Telephone 020 7684 3323
Fax 020 7684 3334
Email info@beam.co.uk
www.beam.co.uk
© BEAM Education 2008, a division of Nelson Thornes
All rights reserved. None of the material in this book may be reproduced in any form without prior permission of the publisher.
ISBN 978 1 874099 65 9
British Library Cataloguing-in-Publication Data
Data available
Edited by Marion Dill
Design by Malena Wilson-Max
Layout by Matt Carr and Roger Marks
Photographs by Judith Stevens,
Len Cross and Ken Wilson-Max
2nd reprint March 2008
Printed in Spain

Contents

Lots of Early Years practitioners just love working with maths and young children, but those who feel less confident about maths than other areas of learning need not despair. Help is at hand! They will find *Maths in Stories* by Judith Stevens a practical resource and a wonderful source of guidance and ideas. In *Maths in Stories*, Judith is looking at the way in which well-known stories and those with which children may be less familiar can be used both as a starting point for adult-planned maths, but also to support and extend activities children initiate.

This book will help practitioners make maths relevant and exciting for the children they work with and so build their confidence in themselves as mathematicians.

Lesley Staggs

Lesley Staggs
Early Childhood Consultant

Chapter 1

Let's start at the very beginning ...

The essence of mathematics is not to make simple things complicated, but to make complicated things simple.

Stanley Gudder

All Early Years practitioners want children to be enthusiastic, curious and motivated when it comes to maths learning, and we as practitioners need to build on their interests and what they already know and can do.

To turn the world of maths into an exciting place to be in, we need to find 'ways into mathematics' for all children and develop a learning environment that supports mathematical thinking. Planning activities and experiences which adults and children alike explore together and identifying the maths learning in simple, hands-on fun activities is an important part of the process.

Books and stories are a valuable resource to help you with this, as they allow children to explore all strands of mathematical development

safely and with confidence. Stories with their range of different characters and settings give mathematical problem solving and thinking a context that seems authentic.

Opening a book is an adventure that can unlock doors to whole new worlds. Listening to stories and sharing books is pleasurable, exciting and fun for all children, and it will provide more opportunities for them to read for themselves. With the help of books and stories, you will turn maths learning into a positive and rewarding experience for children.

Books and stories in the early years

Buying books can be great fun. You can turn it into an outing to a bookshop with the whole group and encourage the children to help you choose books for the collection which can be stored in the home corner or in their classroom library.

Classic as well as modern books help enrich children's learning and have many things in common: the text is memorable, and the illustrations are stimulating; the books are meaningful and relevant to children and often lead to discussion and debate. If the books are exciting and appealing, children (and adults!) will want to revisit them again and again, eventually enabling them to retell the stories independently.

We can build on this by setting up dramatic play to act out the story, leading to more conversations and problem-solving situations that allow mathematical skills and mathematical enquiries to be developed: "How can we find out how many characters there are in this story?"; "Does anyone have an idea of what props we will need?"; "I wonder how large a space we will need for a stage?"; "Do you think it would help to make a list of the characters?" With a small nudge from us, the opportunities for problem solving and mathematical talking are endless as we encourage dramatic play from a favourite story.

Bear in mind that some children – often boys – are more drawn to informative texts than to storybooks. They prefer to gather facts and information from books as part of their own quest to make sense of the world around them. They seek to find out 'why things happen' and 'how things work' and are frequently drawn to books which support their play themes such as as 'monsters', 'diggers and dumpers' or 'dinosaurs'. The knowledge they gather this way makes them feel safe and offers the security that girls often find in storybooks.

As children need easy access to books that fascinate them, both at home and in the school environment, help them find out more about a topic they are interested in and support them in their search for facts or stories. Encourage children to take books and read at home as well.

Finding ways into mathematics

There are lots of wonderful counting books around which are designed to support children's understanding of number. In addition, there are many books in which the maths is easily identifiable and obvious. But you also need to look more closely at familiar fiction and find the maths in unexpected places. It could well be that, initially, a book does not appear to have strong links with mathematics. In that case, you will need to find, and look at, certain aspects that stimulate children's maths interests: for example, a particular character, large or small, could lead to an investigation into size, or a key theme such as 'treasure' or 'gold' could be used to familiarize young children with counting and sorting.

However, it is important that you don't try to make contrived links with maths: not all books and stories will support maths learning and that's fine! Books and stories are there to be enjoyed and cherished. Sometimes, it is simply about the pleasure of exploring language or entering into the fantastic world of make-believe.

The importance of open-ended questioning

From an early age, some young children become quite aware that the questions some adults ask are 'testing questions'. They are often very perceptive and realise that adults already know the answer to questions such as: "How many cars are there in the garage?" or "Which apple is bigger?" They also begin to understand that these closed, testing questions have 'right' and 'wrong' answers. Children who know the answers and are keen to please adults just 'play the game'. Other children, though, may avoid this kind of interaction, which can lead to them not interacting with adults in general. You therefore

need to consider carefully the questions you ask the children in your setting.

If children realise that adults are asking questions because they are actually interested in the answers and that there are no 'wrong' answers, they are likely to interact with you in a more positive way. At first, it may be difficult to include open questions naturally in conversations with children, and you may want to consider for the whole staff team to discuss the type of questions to ask, then display the beginning of these questions around the setting to act as prompts.

Open questions could include the following:

What can we do to remember the number of cakes in the box?

What can we say about the necklaces?

Can you guess how many fruits you can pick up in one hand?

What would happen if the bucket was full?

Can you tell me about the pattern you have made?

What was the first thing you did with the large blocks? And next?

How do you think we could make sure we have enough plates for everyone?

What will you need to make a snake longer than the yellow one?

Which do you think could be the best-sized box for the teddy?

Can you explain why you think those potatoes won't fit in the bag?

Why do you think that ribbon isn't long enough?

Can you think of a way to make sure we all get the same number of strawberries?

What did you notice about the collection of animals?

Can you tell us what is similar about those socks? What is different?

I wonder why the big box feels lighter than the small one?

Problem solving

For children to become confident in the way they express themselves and deal with the manifold challenges they meet in the Early Years setting, it is equally important to model problem-solving strategies and to help children identify problems which are relevant and meaningful to them. Enthusiasm is contagious: if you develop an exciting, challenging learning environment which promotes problem solving, you will automatically create an atmosphere in which children feel able to take risks and 'have a go' without the worry that they might 'be wrong'.

Books at a glance

Well, the good news is that books don't have to be labelled 'maths books' for children to learn maths, and the even better news is that the best books are the ones that children know and love.

To help you get started on your *Maths in Stories* adventure, the list on the next page provides a variety of old-time favourites and modern books you can use in your setting. The first few concentrate on counting, which is a good way to introduce children to the amazing world of number. You will find similar lists throughout the book, to go with certain topics.

Title	Author	Publisher
Five Little Ducks	Ian Beck	Orchard, 1999
One Bear at Bedtime	Mick Inkpen	Hodder, 1989
Ten Little Dinosaurs	Pattie Schnetzler	Accord, 1996
How many Bugs in a Box?	David Carter	Little Simon, 2006
One Moose, 20 Mice	Clare Beeton	Barefoot, 2000
Handa's Hen	Eileen Brown	Walker, 2003
Ten Terrible Dinosaurs	Paul Strickland	Ragged Bears, 2005
Nine Naughty Kittens	Linda Jennings	Little Tiger, 2000
When Sheep cannot Sleep	Satoshi Kitamura	Red Fox, 1998
The Tiger and the Jackal	Vivian French	Walker, 2001
The Old Woman and the Red Pumpkin	Betsy Bang	Walker, 1999
Jamil's Clever Cat	Fiona French	Frances Lincoln, 2000
Mouse Moves House	Nick Sharratt	Candlewick, 2000

The learning environment

Stories are whatever the storyteller or pretend player wishes the story to be.

Helen Williams

As practitioners, we want to establish an environment that promotes mathematical thinking and builds towards becoming a community of learners.

In a learning environment that is stimulating, exciting and offers challenge, children will feel able to follow their own interests and play themes by moving between the areas of provision. Organise the day to give children as much time as possible, within each session, to make their own choices and follow their own interests.

Develop clearly identified spaces or areas of provision, both indoors and outdoors, to support the six areas of learning. These spaces may be called different things, but what is most important is that they do exist and that both adults and children know where to find specific resources or to become involved in certain activities.

It is helpful to label the areas of provision with words and photographs of children involved in the spaces and to identify the independent, child-initiated learning which can occur in each of the areas. It is essential that all areas of provision are:

- carefully planned for
- inviting, stimulating and challenging
- structured and well maintained
- organised to ensure resources are accessible to children and adults

Possible areas of provision
across indoors and outdoors

- Home corner and
  role play
- Creative workshop
- Construction –
  small and large
- Sand
- Water
- Graphics/Writing
- Story telling
- Small-world play/
  Imaginative play
- Music/Sound-making
- Mathematics/Problem
  solving, reasoning and
  numeracy workshop
- ICT

Enriching play environments

There will always be opportunities during children's play to measure, weigh, make number labels, count money, write lists, collect data and sort objects. Children just need the right props to encourage them to incorporate more maths into their play to dramatise the books and stories they have read.

Role-play area

Fill a small suitcase with artefacts that could belong to a story character and encourage the children to discuss who the 'lost' suitcase might belong to.

Construction

Include a range of measuring devices such as metre sticks and T-squares in the construction area as well as clipboards and paper to record the measurements and drawings.

Sand and water

Bury objects in the sand box and let children dig, discover and sort them. Bury dinosaur bones (from a model kit), dig them up and use tapes to measure them and sort them according to length.

Using a tray of water, sieve for jewels and count how many are found.

Making collections

A prop box can also be developed to incorporate collections of different objects which will encourage children to ask questions, make connections and identify problems they want to solve. Put out a few collections at a time, each one separately boxed in an inviting container. Some of your collections might contain:

- Coins
- Socks
- Keys
- Bottles
- Buttons

- Bags, wallets and purses
- Boxes
- Pegs
- Spoons
- Small toys

Developing a maths workshop

A maths workshop should be one part of a workshop approach which supports children's autonomy and independence and encourages them to take control of their own learning. In a setting which has adopted a workshop approach, you can ensure that a wide range of resources is available, enabling children to make independent choices to support their own learning.

The maths workshop should be sited near other areas of provision which complement and extend the learning. This could be near the investigation and exploration area to support sorting, classifying and problem solving or the graphics area to support recording through words, symbols and numerals.

The maths workshop area can be large or small. It is important that practitioners and children know where and how resources are stored. The ideal storage containers are clear or opaque, labelled with words and photographs, so that children know exactly what is in every one. A number reference area should include a meaningful, relevant number line, with picture clues, at child height.

Although specific resources are stored within identified workshop areas, children use them throughout the learning environment, combining resources from different areas to support their play and returning them to the correct location when finished.

Key resources for the maths workshop

The maths resources should be organised so that children can easily identify, transport and use the materials.

The following key resources will help children explore maths:

- Storybooks
- Informative texts
- A clear number line with photographic clues
- A height chart with non-standard measures – possibly handprints
- Commercially produced resources to count, sort, order and classify – bears, elephants, fruit, dinosaurs, frogs
- Natural objects – shells, pebbles, conkers, fir cones, leaves
- Sorting trays, circles, felt squares and laminated coloured card
- Wicker, plastic, metal and wooden bowls
- Wooden, plastic, magnetic and card numerals

- Assorted beads, cotton reels and laces
- Wooden and plastic coloured blocks
- Clipboards and pens for recording
- Number fans
- Tessellating shapes
- Elastic bands and boards
- Sand, tocker and mechanical timers
- Rulers and tape measures
- Balance and scales
- Lotto, dominoes, track and card games
- Abacus
- Calculators
- Assorted puzzles – sequencing, graded, colour, number and shape

Introducing maths into story props

It is important that children have access to props which help them retell stories and rhymes. These can include objects from the story, such as a tea set, plastic food or soft toys and puppets, to use as characters. You can increase the opportunities for maths learning by adding number cards or a number line featuring a character from the book.

Playing with real or authentic props provides a good context for using mathematical language. Prop boxes can be organised into themes such as the vet's box which will contain all the equipment necessary to set up a vet's surgery, together with books and stories about pets. Or the prop box can be linked to one particular story such as *Goldilocks and the Three Bears*. In practice, most people have as many prop boxes as they have storage for organised in themes and books, and resourcing them for maths as well as literacy learning doubles the effectiveness of the boxes.

Magnetic props

Support children in retelling favourite stories and rhymes by using magnetic props. These can be laminated coloured pictures used with magnetic boards or wedges and give children the opportunity to retell the story or to explore familiar rhymes and stories and make up their own. Provide 3D solids such as recycled boxes with magnets attached to be 'houses' for the characters. If the props are taken home, they can be used with a biscuit tin lid, metal tray or be put on the refrigerator door.

Story sacks

Another good idea is to develop a story sack to support core books. Story sacks are generally large cloth bags containing the storybook with supporting materials such as puppets, soft toys, magnetic props, an informative text and a game. There is usually a story tape so that the children can follow along and act out the story. Story sacks are a popular, non-threatening way of encouraging families and the wider community to get involved in supporting their children's learning.

If story sacks are developed for use at home, it is important to include a short guide containing questions to ask, words to introduce, ways of extending sharing the book and how to support early learning. Some sacks will be literacy based, but

it is easy to develop sacks which focus on mathematical learning, too, as well as including some maths props into all the sacks.

A story sack for *Handa's Surprise* by Eileen Browne (Mantra, 1999), for example, could include the book, an informative text about fruit, a set of magnetic story props, fruit-sorting counters, a fruit jigsaw puzzle, plastic fruits, a recording of the story and a simple counting game or fruit lotto.

Story boxes

Story boxes are small worlds created within a shoe box or similar. Children and adults can 'open the box' into new worlds and allow their imagination to roam.

Story boxes, in common with all small-world play and role play, are open ended so that one generic theme can be developed to support many traditional stories or favourite books: for example, forest, underwater, cottage, town, countryside, fairies, parties, treasure. In general, the most usual approach is to cut down two corners of the box to make access more easy and then design a background and floor for the box. This could include 2D drawings or photographs, a collage or textures. Then small props, which usually include people and natural objects, are added. Again, look for ways of developing maths learning, either through props such as tape measures or shapes or through providing props such as birthday badges with a number on that will lead to mathematical discussion.

Children need time to engage in uninterrupted play to explore the many possibilities of the story boxes. Before the children get started, identify the possible mathematical learning. After free play, talk about the play session with the group and ask related questions.

Small-world play

Children develop a wide range of skills and attitudes through imaginative play. Well-planned, open-ended, imaginative small-world play scenarios encourage children to explore imaginary and fantasy worlds which will endlessly fascinate and delight them. Children spend a lot of time making sense of the world around them, and small-world play allows them to revisit real and imagined events and to make sense of the maths they encounter.

Small-world play can be incorporated into sand and water, construction or malleable play. With the children's help, you can arrange scenarios in large or small trays, on tables, floor mats or carpeted areas, which will give a context for the maths, They can be so popular with children that you may want to leave the 'worlds' undisturbed to be revisited over a period of time. This works particularly well for large black builders' trays that can be moved with the contents if necessary.

Be creative when presenting resources in stimulating ways and look for ways to incorporate maths props. A narrow 'grow bag' tray or 'potting' tray on a small table can be transformed into an winter wonderland by the addition of some ice cubes, fake snow, glitter, white gauze, chiffon and lace, flat glass stones, rocks, fir cones, shells, silver gravel and arctic animals.

It is best to develop collections of resources which can be used in a number of ways to support the development of small-world play. Families can be encouraged to contribute to collections of fabrics, scarves, shells, pebbles, plants, mirrors, branches, cones, twigs and rocks. Some resources should be easily accessible to children, so that they can develop their imaginative play independently.

Trays are a core part of small-world provision: some can be purchased from educational suppliers; others are available at garden centres, builders' merchants and pet shops. Cat litter trays, in particular, are fun and come in different sizes, depths and bright colours. In addition, store quantities of natural resources which enhance small-world play: sand, gravel, wood shavings, bark chippings, cocoa shells, pebbles and potting compost. Fake grass and floor mats are alternative options.

Making games from stories

Games provide great opportunities for rehearsing number skills such as counting on and counting back as well as problem-solving scenarios. And when they are set in the context of a book or story that the children are familiar with, they can be especially rich mathematically.

An issue for some young children when they are playing board games is waiting for their turn. You can overcome this to a certain extent by playing in pairs, but a better solution is to use giant dice or a large spinner where everyone can see the numbers and join in, saying the number and counting the jumps that the player, whose turn it is, is making. Most storybooks can be turned into a number-track board game where the events in the story happen along the track, or children can just choose a character from the story to jump along a track. Not all games need to be track games.

How to play 'Pairs' or 'Pelmanism'

You can create a Pelmanism game with either two or four identical characters or images from the story on cards. Depending on the developmental stage of the children, there could be between six pairs or 10 sets of four pictures of foods, animals, toys, wheeled vehicles, dinosaurs, plants and trees, faces, clothes, storybook characters or any other items from the storybook which interest children.

Shuffle the cards and place in rows, face down. Children take turns to turn over two cards. If they match, they keep the pair; if not, they place the cards face down again. Children try to remember where the cards are and find as many pairs as possible. Play continues until all the pairs are discovered. The player with the most pairs is the winner.

How to play 'Kim's game'

'Kim's game' is a simple game which is best played with real objects, but can also be played with photographs or pictures. The idea is that children and adults look at a number of items together and discuss them. For young children, this could be six things; for older children, familiar with the game, it could be a lot more. Everyone tries to remember the items before one is taken out. Children have to guess which item is missing. Using a landscape with plastic insects, for example, and taking away one can be fun as well as challenging.

A working model

The learning environment is only one aspect that encourages mathematical thinking. Another ingredient is the experience and quality of play that we offer, and the activities we devise all contribute to becoming a community of learners.

The play scenarios and the activities in *Maths in Stories* has been inspired by using some of my favourite books to develop children's interest in, and understanding of, maths. There are broadly three different approaches where you can use stories to develop the maths: take a theme such as journeys and use storybooks to support your theme, one of the most popular journey-themed books, of course, being *We're Going on a Bear Hunt*. Fortunately, most storybooks can be loosely grouped by topic or theme. Another way is to focus on a particular book such as *Pants* and use the story as a focus for a range of maths activities. The third approach is to identify a maths idea and use a selection of perhaps unrelated books to develop the maths, the obvious maths learning selection here being counting and a collection of different counting books. Whichever way you organise the children's maths experiences, you can use the activities in this book as a springboard for developing new and stimulating learning opportunities. I have planned every mathematical experience in a similar way. Most identify the following aspects, including links to the maths learning in the Early Years Foundation Stage curriculum.

- Maths learning objectives
- Mathematical vocabulary
- What you will need – resources
- What to do – activities in the setting
- Questions to support mathematical thinking and problem solving
- Other related activities
- Extensions
- A list of books with similar themes

Starting from a theme: Journeys

Journeys are an interesting topic for children, and most will have experienced the buzz and excitement that comes with getting ready for a holiday, going on an outing with the school or with family and friends or a sunny afternoon spent in the park.

Books about journeys are a great way into thinking about the mathematical aspects of shape and space and measures, and young children will be delighted to describe journeys or have fun making maps while they learn about fundamental maths ideas in a playful way.

We're Going on a Bear Hunt

This book by Michael Rosen and Helen Oxenbury (Walker Books, 1989), a real classic, lends itself well to exploring the journey theme, and a simple black tray is the perfect resource for imaginative play.

Maths learning

Contribute to talk about a simple journey

Describe a simple journey

Use everyday words to describe position

Vocabulary

under, over, through, first, second, third, last

You will need:

- A black tray
- A plastic bear in a cave
- Plastic play people
- Tactile resources to represent the journey: sand, 'long grass' turf, cotton wool snow, topsoil 'mud'

What to do:

* Set up the black tray with areas to represent the journey the family undertake on their bear hunt.
* Provide a 'cave' (papier mâché onto a small cardboard box is ideal). You can create the cave in advance, together with the children.
* Support the children as they retell the story using positional language.

Questions to support mathematical thinking and problem solving:

Can you tell me about your journey?

How do you think we could explain where we went?

Which do you think could be the best way to get from home to the cave?

Can you think of a way to make the journey shorter?

Making plans and maps

At times, moving on from the 'concrete' of 3D props to the abstract of 2D symbolic maps is not an easy process for young children. Help children with the process by supporting the making of 'plans'. Aim to provide wooden houses, trees, road signs, other buildings and small-world resources such as playground equipment, which appear in favourite books. Encourage the children to lay these out on a large piece of A1 paper or lining paper. Discuss what features are 'next to', 'close to' and 'far away' from each other. Make digital images of the town/village. Then take one feature away at a time, supporting children to record what was there with 2D pictures/symbols. Spend time describing routes from one feature to another.

Discuss the plan together and add in other features such as roads, car parks and parks. Where possible, laminate the plan or place under clear acetate. Support the children as they use this as an imaginative play mat.

Books with a journey theme

Title	Author	Publisher
The Train Ride	June Crebbin	Walker, 1996
Mr Gumpy's Outing	John Burningham	Jonathan Cape, 2000
Oi! Get off our Train	John Burningham	Red Fox, 1991
A Balloon for Grandad	Nigel Gray	Orchard, 2002
Rosie's Walk	Pat Hutchins	Red Fox, 2001
The Mystery of the Blue Arrows	Chuck McKee	Anderson, 1990
Follow the Line	Simone Lia	Egmont, 2002
We're Going on a Lion Hunt	David Axtell	MacMillan, 2000

Starting from a book: Pants

The most delightful aspect of *Pants* by Giles Andreae (Picture Corgi, 2003) is that it plays on children's fascination with underpants of all shapes and sizes. It gives them opportunities to explore shapes, patterns and size and have fun at the same time.

Maths learning

Talk about size, patterns and colours

Look closely at similarities and differences

Use vocabulary such as 'bigger' and 'smaller'

Vocabulary

pattern, size, too big, too small, bigger than, smaller than, the same as, different from

You will need:

- A wicker laundry basket
- Pants in assorted sizes and colours

What to do:

❊ Introduce and reinforce the use of specific vocabulary.

❊ Encourage the children to explore the pants, discuss them, notice similarities and differences, patterns and colours.

❊ Support the children as they predict which pants will fit them and try them on to find out if they are correct.

Questions to support mathematical thinking and problem solving:

Can you guess how many pants there are in the basket?

Which do you think could be the biggest?

Can you think of a way to sort the pants?

Other related activities:

❊ Sort shoes and boots.

❊ Explore hats and hat boxes.

Books with a clothes theme:

Title	Author	Publisher
Washing Line	Jez Alborough	Walker, 1999
Mrs Mopple's Washing Line	Anita Hewitt	Red Fox, 1996
Mrs Lather's Laundry	Allan Ahlberg	Golden Press, 1982

Starting from maths learning: Counting

Matching socks

Children who have had experience of counting and knowing number names to 10 will become more confident in handling larger numbers if you give them lots of opportunities to count a wide range of objects, supported by visually exciting counting books.

You will need:

- A wicker laundry basket
- Assorted pairs of socks and pegs
- A washing line at child height

What to do:

❉ Encourage the children to explore the socks and support them as they find the matching pairs.

❉ Ask the children to explain the criteria they have chosen.

❉ Support children when they begin to count in twos.

Questions to support mathematical thinking and problem solving:

Can you guess how many socks there are altogether? How can we check?

If there are 12 socks, how many pairs do you think you can make?

Which do you think could be the smallest?

Can you find two socks which are similar? Can you tell us why?

Maths learning

Count and match pegs and socks

Identify pairs using pattern, colour or size

Count aloud in twos

Vocabulary

count, numbers, match, the same as, in twos, pairs, same size, larger, smaller, pattern

Books with a counting theme:

Title	Author	Publisher
How Many Sharks in the Bath?	Bill Gillham/ Jez Alborough	Frances Lincoln, 2006
1, 2, 3 to the Zoo	Eric Carle	Grosse and Dunlap, 2007
How Many Peas in a Pod?	Margaret Allum	Little Hare, 2005
One Gorilla	Atsuko Morozumi	Matthew Price, 2006

Chapter 3

Storybooks and picture books

*Can you do Division? Divide a loaf by a knife – what's the answer
to that? Bread-and-butter, of course.*

Lewis Carroll

There are many fantastic storybooks and
picture books on the market, and you
will want to introduce new books and
stories on a regular basis. Children
need to hear stories for their own sake,
for pleasure and enjoyment. This is
motivational in itself and provides a
context for mathematical exploration.

Storybooks and picture books are an
ideal focus for a maths conversation.
In the right hands, picture books have
the potential to expose children to
mathematical illustrations and language. Children find it more 'normal'
to use maths vocabulary in the context of a picture-book discussion than
in a more forced question-and-answer situation. Discussions that start
with "I wonder what", "I wonder if" or "Do you think that" questions will
give rise to a richer mathematical conversation, as will questions such
as "I can't see where the little black cat is hiding ... can you?" that help
children become involved in mathematical discussions.

When introducing new stories, read or tell the complete story and discuss
some key elements, which could be about certain characters, a journey in
the book or significant incidents. Support children's independent retelling
of stories by using story props, puppets, magnetic props, story boxes or
small-world play scenarios.

Our pets

In any group of children there is always a large majority who are fascinated by animals or those who are desperate for a cat, dog or hamster, so a pets theme is popular. It provides a focus for collecting data and endless weighing and measuring.

The Great Pet Sale

One of the best things about *The Great Pet Sale* by Mick Inkpen (Hodder Children's Books, 1999) is the rat with one whisker that appears on every page. He does everything he can to gain the attention of the child choosing a pet. The book stimulates discussion about size, money and shopping.

Identifying pets – adult-directed activity

Maths learning

Use language such as 'too big' and 'too small'

Use everyday words to describe shape

Use the vocabulary of money

Vocabulary

coin, penny, sale, buy, how much?, money, cost, not enough, more than, less than, too big, too small, longer, wider

You will need:

- Assorted soft toys or puppets and a rubber rat with one whisker in a sack
- Sticky labels and marker pens
- Coins
- Pet-carrying boxes

What to do:

* Remind the children of the characters in the book.
* Show the children the sack and ask them to guess what is in it. Ask one child to feel inside the sack and describe what they can feel, then take the item out of the sack and show it to the other children. Continue in the same way until the children have found all the pets.
* Discuss how to remember which pets have been taken out of the sack.
* Encourage the children to make price labels for the pets.
* Support the children as they use the coins to buy and sell the animals and find a carry box the right size.

Questions to support mathematical thinking and problem solving:

Can you guess what is in this bag? What does it feel like?

What can we do to show people the price of the pets?

How do you think we could make sure the pet will fit in the box?

I wonder which could be the biggest pet?

What did you notice about the boxes?

Can you tell us what is similar about those pets? What is different?

The 'Feeding the dogs' game

A popular activity with young children and perfect for counting, recognising numerals and guessing and estimating.

You will need:

- Four soft-toy dogs
- Bone-shaped, hard dog biscuits or bone-shaped salt dough biscuits in a wicker basket
- A 1–3 dice
- Four dog bowls

What to do:

✳ Encourage the children to choose a dog and bowl each.

✳ Support them as they throw the dice and count out the correct number of bones from the basket into their own dog bowl.

✳ Continue until all the bones have gone from the basket. Predict who has the most and estimate how many each player has. Count together to check.

Maths learning

Count to three objects by saying one number name for each item

Recognise numerals 1 to 3

Estimate

Compare two groups of objects, saying when they have the same number

Vocabulary

how many?, more, left, add, less than, more than, the same as, total, guess, predict, estimate

Other related activities:

❋ Build a kennel for a specific-sized dog from construction equipment or empty boxes.

❋ Create simple, repeating patterns on narrow strips of paper to make a dog collar.

❋ Fit different-sized zoo animals into boxes.

❋ Count or sort plastic animals.

A new puppy – child-initiated play

Consider adding a new pet dog to the home corner, with resources which support mathematical development:

Dog collars of different sizes

Feeding bowls of different sizes/colours

Empty dog-biscuit boxes

Hard dog biscuits to sort or count

Balance to weigh dog biscuits

Feeding instructions – how many biscuits and when

Dog passport – name, age, weight

Vet's card – date, age, weight, number of pills

Other bigger and smaller 'pets'

Carry boxes – too small, too big, and so on

Alarm clock – for feeding times and times for walks

Other books with a pets theme:

Title	Author	Publisher
Dear Zoo	Rod Campbell	Simon & Schuster, 2005
Six-Dinner Sid	Inga Moore	Simon & Schuster, 1993
My Cat Likes to Hide in Boxes	Eve Sutton	Parents' Magazine Press, 1974
Mog's Family of Cats	Judith Kerr	Collins, 2003

Making the most of shopping and food

Books about shopping provide the opportunity to discuss money and to talk about counting, calculation and measures. Before you plan activities around shopping, have a discussion with the group to find out about children's shopping experiences. You could discuss ideas such as the differences between shopping in a small shop and a large supermarket. Invite comments about the procedure for ordering goods on the Internet.

The Shopping Basket

The maths in *The Shopping Basket* by John Burningham (Red Fox, 1992) is all about handling money and listening and following directions. Children will be fascinated by the opening page, where Steven, who is at the market, is being confronted by an elephant!

A shopping game

You will need:

- The book
- Doubles of all the items from *The Shopping Basket*
- Photos of the correct number of items on two pieces of A3 card
- Cards with photos of the items and a cloth bag
- A dice with 1 on three sides and 2 on the other three sides

What to do:

※ Discuss the photos on the A3 cards with the children.

※ Put the small cards in a cloth bag and support the children as they take turns to choose a card and throw the dice. If they throw a 2 and pick a banana card, they place two bananas on the first A3 card.

※ The game continues until the A3 cards are filled up. However, if all the oranges on one card are full and the child picks an orange and gets a 2 when rolling the dice, they have to give the two oranges to the other child.

※ Continue until one A3 card is completely full.

Questions to support mathematical thinking and problem solving:

How many do you think you need to make 5?

Can you explain why you think you need one more to make 6?

I wonder if there are the same number of bananas and oranges?

Maths learning

Count up to three objects by saying one number name for each item

Willingly attempt to count

Recognise groups with one, two or three objects

Find the total number of items in two groups by counting all of them

---

Vocabulary

how many?, more, left, add, less than, more than, the same as, total, guess, predict, estimate

Baskets and bags – child-initiated play

Baskets and bags are excellent resources to help introduce estimation and measures: "How many small cereal boxes to you think will fit into this basket?"; "Which bag is heavier now that it's full of apples – this one or that one?"

You will need:

- Assorted shopping baskets and shopping bags
- Small-, medium- and large-sized shiny and sparkly gift bags
- Real vegetables such as potatoes, carrots, turnips, parsnips, sweet potatoes, courgettes

What to do:

❋ Support the children as they sort the bags or food and explain the criteria they have used.

❋ Introduce and model the use of the language of size.

❋ Encourage the children to predict how many vegetables will fit in each bag and then count to check.

Questions to support mathematical thinking and problem solving:

Which do you think is the biggest bag?

Do you think the sweet potato will fit into the smallest bag?

I wonder which is the best-sized bag for 10 potatoes?

Can you guess how many carrots will fit into the blue bag?

What will you need to carry all the vegetables?

Maths learning

Use developing mathematical ideas to solve practical problems

Willingly attempt to count, with some numbers in the correct order

Compare two different groups and predict which is 'more' or 'less'

Predict whether an object will fit into a certain size container

---

Vocabulary

full, empty, more than, less than, bigger than, smaller than

Coins – adult-initiated activity

Using real money lets children explore a real-life situation during creative and stimulating imaginative play.

You will need:

- Assorted coins and paper money from around the world
- Money boxes, purses and wallets

What to do:

- Introduce and model the use of money and shopping.
- Observe the children's play and extend where appropriate.
- Join in children's conversations about earlier experiences.

Questions to support mathematical thinking and problem solving:

What was the first thing you did when you saw the coins?

Can you tell me why you put those coins together in the purse?

How do you think we could share out the coins?

Which do you think could be the most valuable coin? Why?

Can you explain why you think the biggest coin can buy more toys?

Can you tell us what is similar about those two notes? What is different?

Maths learning
Recognise numerals to 10
Use some number names accurately in play
Use the language of addition in play
Match numerals in imaginative or role play

Vocabulary
coin, money, note, cost, amount, purse, wallet, total, change, penny, pence, pound, dollar, cent, euro, pay, buy, shop, shopping, cash, full, empty

---

Bank boxes

Resource the number area with a collection of money boxes or shoe boxes with a slit in the lid and a dish of small coins. Place a notice next to every box saying what coin can be put in the box. Tell children to take a handful of coins and put each coin into the right box. Ask 'coin checkers' to tip out the contents of every box and check that all the coins are the same.

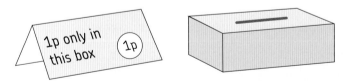

Can you tell me the name of this coin?
I wonder what box I can put the 5p coin in?

Shopping lists

Making shopping lists will encourage young children to experiment with written numbers and numerals and allow them to practise mathematical language.

You will need:

- A simple writing framework
- Multiples of real foods and empty packets: for example, baked bean tins, tomatoes, carrots, kiwis, cereal boxes, crisp packets, and so on
- Assorted graphical media

What to do:

❋ Design a simple shopping list on a PC. Try to make it look like a real note-pad shopping list, with pictures of fruit, vegetables or a shopping basket/trolley. Include lines for children to write on. Differentiate the framework so that those children who are more confident with writing can write the number and the item. For less confident children, include the words, leaving gaps for numerals.

❋ Encourage the children to choose four or five items for their list, count the number of each and write the numeral.

Questions to support mathematical thinking and problem solving:

Can you tell me what you would like to buy at the shops?

How do you think we could record what you want to buy?

What can we do to make sure we don't forget anything?

Can you think of a way to make sure we get the right amount of baked beans?

Can you tell us what is similar about the tins? What is different?

What was the first thing you did when you wrote your list?

Maths learning

Know that the answer to the question 'how many?' will be a number

Willingly attempt to count, with some numbers in the correct order

Write some numerals

Know that the last number said is the number of objects in the group

---

Vocabulary

heavier, lighter, smaller, bigger, cost, money, number, price, count, one, two, three, list, amount, shopping

Sorting fruits

You will need:

- A set of different kinds of fruit
- A large wooden fruit bowl and plastic fruit bowls in different colours or paper bowls with photos of real fruit
- Cut-out hand prints stuck onto card and laminated

What to do:

❋ Encourage the children to explore the fruits independently, find similarities and differences, count, calculate and talk about, recognise and recreate simple patterns.

❋ Support the children as they predict how many pieces of fruit they can pick up and then grab as many fruit as possible in one hand, counting together to confirm. Place the fruits on the hand prints to support the children as they count, using fingers. Encourage them to predict how many they can pick up with the other hand and try it and see: "Why do you think there are more kiwis than pears? Or less?"

❋ Observe the children's play and ask open questions which encourage children to talk about what they are doing, and why.

Questions to support mathematical thinking and problem solving:

Can you guess how many fruits you can pick up with one hand?

What can we do to check?

Can you guess how many fruits you can pick up with the other hand?

Why do you think there are less?

Can you tell me about the pattern you have created?

Can you explain why you think that an orange comes next in the pattern?

Maths learning

Solve number problems in practical everyday situations, using real objects

Create a pattern, using real objects

Count reliably to 10 everyday objects

Use everyday words to describe position

Vocabulary

pattern, the same as, different, repeat, continue, create, sort

Making the most of real fruit and vegetables

❊ Consider growing vegetables from seeds and beans: look at the size and shapes, measure the growth and finally taste the produce.

❊ Explore the vegetables, looking at size, shape, colour, numbers, similarities and differences. Chop the vegetables into pieces, compare the sizes and shapes, estimate how many pieces can be grabbed by one hand, then count them.

❊ Make a block graph, showing children's favourite vegetables or fruit after tasting several.

❊ Explore satsumas, mandarins or oranges. Estimate how many segments could be in one. Count and see! Are there more or less in the next fruit? How many are there altogether?

❊ Estimate the number of bananas in a bunch: look at the size, shape and colour. Are all bananas the same?

❊ Make fruit kebabs: create repeating patterns using banana, grapes, mango, peach, strawberries or other seasonal fruits.

❊ Play the 'potato game' outdoors. With the children, lay down four lines with six large potatoes in each. Place a bucket at one end of the line. Children take turns to start at one end, run or hop to the first potato, collect it and put it in the bucket. The game continues until each potato is collected and placed in the bucket. Children then count out the potatoes and start again.

Other books with a shopping/food theme:

Title	Author	Publisher
The Green Banana Hunt	Jennifer Bent	Scholastic, 1995
When We Go Shopping	Nick Butterworth	HarperCollins, 1994
Tom and Pippo Go Shopping	Helen Oxenbury	Simon & Schuster, 1989
Don't Forget the Bacon	Pat Hutchins	Sagebrush Education, 1989
Eat up, Gemma!	Sarah Hayes	Sagebrush Education, 1994
Lima's Red Hot Chilli Pepper	David Mills	Mantra, 1999
The Very Hungry Caterpillar	Eric Carle	Puffin, 1994
Ruby's Dinner Time	Paul Rogers	Orchard, 2002
We're Going on a Picnic	Pat Hutchins	Red Fox, 2003

Making the most of presents and parties

Young children love parties and birthdays! It is no accident that the first numeral many children recognise is '4'. On their third birthday, they are often not yet interested in numerals, but by their fourth, they are fascinated with cards and badges showing they are '4'. Books about birthdays and parties also offer lots of opportunities to plan mathematical experiences such as exploring 3D solids while wrapping presents.

However, you will need to be aware of the children who do not celebrate birthdays.

Spot's Birthday / Spot's Birthday Party

Both these *Spot* books by Eric Hill (Picture Puffin, 1991 / 1987) are wonderful examples how fun and maths learning can be integrated. Children love the vivacious pup and can identify with Spot and his experiences as he is an early learner, too.

Wrapping presents

You will need:

- Lots of assorted wrapping paper
- Sticky tape
- Ribbons, bows
- Markers
- Gift tags
- Toys

What to do:

❊ Display the toys attractively and add the wrapping paper, decorations and sticky tape.

❊ Encourage the children to choose one toy which they want to wrap as a pretend gift for a friend.

❊ Take turns to predict which paper will be the correct size for the gift. Discuss the colours and patterns on paper. Wrap the toy together.

❊ Select an appropriate length of ribbon and ask the children: "Is it long enough? Is it too short?"

Maths learning

Begin to use the appropriate vocabulary of measures

Use non-standard measures to make comparisons

Order two or three items by length

Write some numerals

Use developing mathematical ideas to solve practical problems

---

Vocabulary

size, length, big, small, bigger than, big enough, too small, fit, cover

❋ Finally, support each individual child to write the age and name of the child the toy is meant for.

❋ Later, have a grand present-giving ceremony, where children take turns to feel their parcel and predict the contents before ripping off the paper!

Questions to support mathematical thinking and problem solving:

Which do you think could be the best-sized paper for the teddy bear?

How do you think we could check?

Can you explain why you think that ribbon is long enough to go around the parcel?

Why do you think it isn't long enough?

What was the first thing you did when you tried to wrap the wooden blocks?

Can you guess what's in the parcel? How can we find out?

Birthday card maths

You will need:

- A selection of birthday cards with numerals 3, 4, 5
- Assorted coloured card, scissors, markers
- Sequins, glitter, shiny paper
- Pictures from magazines
- Assorted-sized envelopes
- A special soft toy that 'has a birthday'

What to do:

- ❊ Take some time to look at the cards together and discuss them.
- ❊ Talk about the toy's birthday and discuss how old the toy might be – explain that no one is quite sure. Why could that be?
- ❊ Support each child to design and make a birthday card for the birthday toy, choosing to write the numeral for the age they think the toy is.
- ❊ Help the children select an appropriate-sized envelope for the card.
- ❊ Later, at group time, take turns to open the cards. Select one child to hold all the cards with the same numeral on. At the end, ask children to predict who has the most cards: "Are there more '4's than '3's? Count the number of cards together to confirm. Whoever has the most cards becomes the age of the toy!"

Questions to support mathematical thinking and problem solving:

Can you guess how old Hedgehog is?

Can you tell me why you think he's three?

Why do you think nobody really knows how old he is?

What will you need to make a card for Hedgehog?

What was the first thing you did when you designed the card?

What would happen if six people think he is five and six people think he is four? Is that fair?

Maths learning

Understand the difference between a letter and a numeral

Match numerals

Recognise some numerals of personal significance

Write some numerals of personal significance

Vocabulary

age, how old?, older, younger, older than, younger than, numeral, number, big enough, too small, more than, less than, most, least

Birthday cakes and candles

You will need:

- Cooked play dough in two colours (maybe with added glitter or sequins)
- Rolling pins, assorted cutters
- Cake cases, bun tins and paper party plates
- Cake decorations, birthday candles and candle holders

What to do:

❋ Arrange the resources in an attractive way.

❋ Encourage the children to roll out the dough, cut out cakes and biscuits, decorate them and add the candles.

❋ Support the children's imaginative role play about birthdays and parties.

Questions to support mathematical thinking and problem solving:

What can we do to share the dough fairly between the cake cases?

Can you guess how many cakes we can make from the pink dough?

How do you think we could make sure everyone gets the same number of cakes?

Can you think of a way to make more cakes from the pink dough?

What will you need to decorate all the cakes?

What would happen if you put five candles on this cake and four on the other cake?

A birthday box

Consider developing a 'birthday box' which can be added to the home corner on occasions to enhance role play. Add to the box throughout the year, discarding some resources and adding new ones. Suitable items are a plastic/paper party table cover; paper plates, cups and napkins; wrapping paper, ribbons and gift tags; salt dough cakes; a birthday banner; invitations; birthday cards.

Other books with a birthday theme:

Title	Author	Publisher
Kipper's Birthday	Mike Inkpen	Sagebrush Education, 2000
Look Out! It's the Wolf!	Emile Jadoule	Zero to Ten/Evans Publishing Group, 2004
Alfie and the Birthday Surprise	Shirley Hughes	Lothrup, Lee & Shephard, 1998
Mog's Amazing Birthday Caper	Judith Kerr	Collins Picture Lion, 1989
Danny's Birthday	Mike Dickinson	Little Hippo, 2000
A Quiet Night in	Jill Murphy	Candlewick Press, 1994

Chapter 4

The bear necessities – all about bears

Teddies go everywhere and do everything.

Margaret Hutchings

Bears have fascinated children for generations. No amount of interactive, high-tech toys can draw attention away from the special cuddly toys in every child's life. That's probably why there are so many wonderful picture books which feature bears as characters in all shapes and sizes. Some appear as toys themselves; others are given human characteristics and live in homes just like ours.

All of the books featured are perennial favourites and can be part of a theme about bears that will intrigue young children for a long time.

Obviously, there are many links to traditional stories such as *Goldilocks and the Three Bears*, and you can adapt the model for the activities in the setting according to the children's needs.

In terms of maths, matching and counting objects, talking about size and sorting objects by maths properties are among the learning experiences in tales and stories about bears.

Permeate the atmosphere with problem solving and bear enquiry during which mathematical skills and concepts can be developed.

Sorting teddies – child-initiated play

A teddies' display is a good way of introducing young children to problem solving, reasoning and numeracy.

You will need:

- Assorted teddies
- Teddy bear wrapping paper
- Teddy bear fabric
- 30 cm ruler or short stick stuck into a piece of modelling dough

Maths learning

Use own criteria to sort objects

Order three objects by height

Use size language such as 'big' and 'small'

Use descriptive language

Vocabulary

big, bigger, biggest, small, smaller, smallest, bigger than, smaller than, taller than, shorter than

What to do:

✳ Cover the top of a small table or low storage unit with teddy bear fabric. Cover the wall or display board behind with teddy bear wrapping paper. Place a few teddies on the display and encourage children to bring more teddies from home.

✳ Introduce and reinforce the use of the language of size.

✳ Encourage the children to sort or order the bears and explain the criteria they have used.

Questions to support mathematical thinking and problem solving:

Can you tell me about your favourite teddy?

Can you explain why you think the blue bear would be Kelly's favourite?

What did you notice about the bears?

Can you tell us what is similar about those two bears? What is different?

What can we say about the brown bears?

What would happen if one of the teddies got lost?

Sorting bears by height – adult-initiated activity

Put out hoops labelled 'bears taller than the stick', 'bears shorter than the stick' and 'bears that are the same height as the stick'.
Ask the children to decide whether or not their bear is taller or shorter than the stick and then put the bear in the appropriate hoop.

Bear buckets – adult-initiated activity

Number lines can be a key part of a number reference area. Apart from using commercial number lines, you could create a number line with a set of 10 buckets which you can change as soon as it loses its appeal.

You will need:

- 55 assorted small sorting bears in a container
- 10 small buckets
- Washing line
- 1–10 number cards

What to do:

❖ Put the bears in a container and the cards on the table, face down.

❖ Each child takes a turn to turn over a card and say the numeral. Children then count the correct number of bears into a bucket and fix the card on the front of the bucket.

❖ When all the buckets are complete, support the children as they peg them in the correct order to a washing line at child height.

Questions to support mathematical thinking and problem solving:

Can you say which number might be on the card? Why can't it be a 6 or a 3?

Can you tell me which number comes next?

How do you think we could make sure these are in the right order?

Can you explain why you think we need two more bears if we have three and we need five altogether?

Which numbers do you think could come between the 5 and the 8?

Maths learning

Recognise 1–10 numerals

Place 1–10 numerals in the correct order

Count to 10 objects by saying one number name for each item

Say number names in order in familiar contexts

Vocabulary

0–10 number names, one less, one more, number line, count

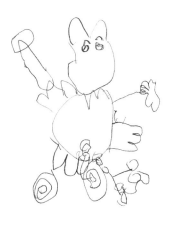

Extensions:

- Keep children interested by changing number lines on a regular basis. Consider using photos of children or pictures linked to bear themes.
- Provide a fixed number line with duplicate cards for children to match and order.
- Use chalk paint to draw a bear track in the outdoor area and play 'jumping along the track' games.

Three bears' interactive display – child-initiated play

Goldilocks and the Three Bears is ideal in the Foundation Stage to illustrate comparing size, matching, sorting and sequencing. It also gives children the chance to describe and explain what happens first and to predict what happens next.

You will need:

- Three teddy bears
- Three spoons and three bowls in assorted sizes
- Bear wrapping paper
- *Goldilocks and the Three Bears* book
- Empty porridge carton
- Children's drawings of three bears
- Speech bubbles and markers
- Numeral '3' in plastic, wood and cardboard

What to do:

- ✳ Cover a display board and storage cupboard top with bear wrapping paper and/or bright fabric.
- ✳ Display the children's drawings of three bears, the book and the story props.
- ✳ Encourage the children to investigate the display and support them as they use descriptive and comparative vocabulary or count the bears.
- ✳ Act as a scribe to record the children's use of mathematical language.

Maths learning

Count up to three objects by saying one number name for each item

Use size language such as 'big', 'small' and 'little'

Compare heights or lengths without measuring

Order three items by size

Vocabulary

big, bigger, biggest, small, smaller, smallest, bigger than, smaller than

Questions to support mathematical thinking and problem solving:

Can you guess which bowl could have the most porridge in?

Can you explain why you think that is Daddy Bear's spoon?

Why do you think did Baby Bear like porridge best?

Can you tell us what is similar about the bowls? What is different?

What can we say about the spoons?

What would happen if you tried to sit on Baby Bear's chair?

Talking of Goldilocks, let's look at an alternative version of an old favourite by Jan Fearnley (Egmont, 2001);

Mr Wolf and the Three Bears

In this twist on a traditional tale, Mr Wolf plans a great party for Baby Bear's birthday. He works with Grandma Wolf to plan the menu, with the three bears' favourite foods top of the list. Everything is going fine until Goldilocks (who is too rough and cheats at 'Musical chairs') turns up. But children will be delighted at the end of the tale.

The book is full of superb ideas for extending mathematics across numbers as labels and for counting, calculating, shape and space and measures:

* Use the recipes in the book, which have clear pictorial instructions and numerals to explore together, to bake a birthday cake, Daddy Bear's huff puffs, Grandma's golden pie or cheesy snip-snap biscuits.

* Write a shopping list for additional party food with prices and go shopping at a local store.

* Discuss how many sandwiches are needed for the party and calculate how many slices of bread are needed. Make the sandwiches and explore halves and quarters, squares and triangles.

* Divide the mixture for the huff puffs fairly between 12 cake cases:

How can we make sure it is fair?

✳ Create a repeating pattern to decorate a hat for the party.

✳ Choose some birthday gifts and predict how much paper is needed to wrap each:
How much ribbon is needed to go around the middle of each one?
Which one do you think will need the most? Which one will need the least?
Which ribbon is the longest? Which is the shortest?

✳ Lay the table:
One paper plate, cup, serviette for each guest. How many do we need?
If we have six guests and four plates, how many more do we need?
We have six guests and 12 huff puffs. How many each?
What will happen when Goldilocks arrives – how many does everyone get then? Is that fair?

✳ Decorate real or playdough cakes:
How many decorations are there?
What patterns could we make with the silver balls and sugar flowers?
Are there enough candles on the cake?
We have two and Baby Bear is four – how many more do we need?
Now there are six candles on the cake, how many do we need to take away?

✳ Play 'Musical chairs':
There are 20 children. How many chairs do we need so that everyone can sit down? If there are 12 still in the game and only 10 chairs left, how many children will be out?

✳ Draw maps with key features, describing the journey to each other:
Describe the journey from the three bears' house to the party at Mr Wolf's house. What did they see? What did they walk past?

- Play hide-and-seek: hide from each other or hide a teddy bear to be found. Use positional language to guide the children to the bear.
- Use a simple writing framework emphasising numerals:

Please come to:

Little Bear's Party

At: ... Fairytale Lane

On: Saturday ...th March

At: ... o'clock

Love from

Daddy Bear x

The 'Bears move house' game

This game is really good for involving children in counting and using their developing problem-solving skills.

You will need:

- A collection of assorted, different-sized bears
- 20 paw prints cut from black paper or card
- 2 boxes large enough to contain the bears
- A large 1–6 dice

What to do:

❋ Put all the bears in one box.

❋ Arrange the paw prints in a long line, starting from the box.

❋ Put the second box at the end of the line.

❋ Take turns to throw the dice and move one of the bears along the paw-print track. Keep taking turns until all the bears have moved from the house box along the track to the other house box.

Maths learning

Count along track

Recognise numerals to 6

Solve practical problems by deciding what bear to move along the track

Vocabulary

one, two ... six, count along, how many?, altogether

Post a teddy

This activity is particularly linked to the picture book *When the Teddy Bears Came* by Martin Waddell (Walker Books, 1994).

Maths learning

Compare lengths without measuring

Predict whether an object will fit into a certain size container

Cut materials to size

Use developing mathematical ideas and methods to solve practical problems

Vocabulary

size, big, bigger, biggest, big enough, too small, long, short, shorter, shortest, too short, number

You will need:

- Assorted toy teddy bears
- Different-sized pieces of brown paper
- String
- Sticky tape
- Scissors
- Gift tags
- Assorted boxes
- Stamps
- Sticky labels

What to do:

✳ Encourage the children to select a bear, predict which size box the bear will fit into and then try it and see.

✳ Then predict the size of the paper needed to wrap the box. Wrap the box together, cutting the paper if necessary, discussing the length of pieces of tape and string.

✳ Support the children as they write address labels, emphasising the numbers for house and post codes and on the stamps.

Questions to support mathematical thinking and problem solving:

Which do you think could be the best box for the fluffy teddy?

Can you explain why you think that teddy will fit into the small box?

How do you think we could fit the teddy in the box?

Can you think of a way to wrap the box in that piece of paper?

Do you think it makes any difference which way up the box is?

What was the first thing you did when you wrapped the box?

Send your bear on holiday

Decide whether the bears are going to a hot or cold country for their holiday. Discuss and make a list of the sort of things they might want while they are away. Look at a map and identify where they might go. Resource an area with travel brochures for the bears to choose a holiday venue and discuss prices and distances.

* Pack a suitcase or bag for your bear to take on holiday.

* Make a passport for your bear: include a picture of your bear (drawn or photograph) and the bear's dimensions such as height, girth and weight.

* Provide a collection of postcards and 'stamps' for the bears to send from their holiday.

* Design a beach towel for your bear, using the computer and a selection of shapes.

* Draw a pattern on your bear's surfboard or snowboard.

* Make some sunglasses and a beach hat for your bear.

A teddy bears' picnic

As a celebration of a theme about bears, consider planning a teddy bears' picnic with the children. Use a book with a picnic theme as a starting point and introduce the song 'If you go down to the woods today'. Discuss the idea of a picnic with the children and sit down together to plan the event. This could include:

• Children designing and making picnic invitations for each other, their teddies or family members, to include the date and time of the picnic

• Making name and address labels, with phone numbers, on luggage labels for their own bear (in case they get lost!)

• Planning the number of sandwiches needed, writing shopping lists, buying ingredients and making sandwiches

• Exploring packets of jelly, discussing the size, shape and number of cubes, reading instructions, measuring the amount of water and making the jelly in moulds

● Discussing picnic rugs, with children guessing how many fit on one rug, then trying it to see and working together to discuss how many rugs are needed altogether. They check if all the rugs are the same size and think about what would happen if adults were sitting on some rugs: "Will we need more rugs in that case?"

● Making maps for the venue if going to the park

And it doesn't matter if it rains – as the bear says in *This is the Bear and the Picnic Lunch*: "Haven't you guessed? Indoor picnics are the best!"

More mathematical bear activities

◆ Make pairs of bear ears. Decide how many pairs you need, then pretend to be the bear.

◆ Decorate bear biscuits (from most supermarkets) with icing pens or use the pens to draw a bear on plain biscuits.

◆ On a block graph, fill in what your bear likes to eat.

◆ Vote for your bear's favourite story and decide which story has the most votes.

◆ Count along with your bear and see how far you can get.

◆ Arrange all bears in a line in height order.

◆ Make a bear height chart. Give children an A5 piece of card to draw their favourite bear on and support them to write one number on each card. Laminate each card and fix together to create a height chart. Encourage children to compare their heights, using the bears as non-standard measures.

◆ Make a bear tape measure. Draw one small bear, photocopy onto different-coloured paper and cut out. With the children, create a repeating pattern on a long strip of narrow paper. Encourage the children to use the non-standard tape to measure familiar objects: "How many bears high do you think the chair is?"

◆ Consider the sorts of footprints bear might make. Make pairs of prints, left and right, and make tracks across the floor: "How many bear strides is it from the home corner to the book corner?"; "Is it more or less than from the garden door to the water tray?"

◆ Consider transforming the whole learning environment into a 'bear hunt': hang white drapes from the ceiling to create a 'snow storm', add wet topsoil to the sand tray to create mud, provide straw in a builders' tray to represent the tall grass and build a bear's cave in the book corner for the bear.

Other books with a bear theme:

Title	Author	Publisher
The Biggest Bear	Adam Relf	Scholastic, 2005
The Grizzly Bear Family Book	Michio Hoshino	Chronicle, 2004
It's the Bear!	Jez Alborough	Walker, 2004
The Biggest Bear	Adam Relf	Scholastic, 2005
We're Going on a Bear Hunt	Michael Rosen	Walker, 1993 Walker, 1993
Can't you Sleep, Little Bear?	Martin Waddell	Walker, 2004
Who wants an Old Teddy Bear?	Ginnie Hofmann	Reverie, 2003
Bartholomew Bear	Virginia Miller	Walker, 2000
Peace at Last	Jill Murphy	MacMillan, 1995
Where's my Teddy?	Jez Alborough	Walker, 2004
Katie Morag and the Tiresome Ted	Mairi Hedderwick	Red Fox, 1999
Big Bear, Little Bear	David Bedford	Little Tiger Press, 2006
Dear Bear	Joanna Harrison	Picture Lions, 1999
This is the Bear and the Picnic Lunch	Sarah Hayes	Walker, 2003

Chapter 5

Counting books

One, two, three, four, five – Once I caught a fish alive!

Traditional English rhyme

In addition to the many excellent storybooks that can be used as starting points for maths, there is a large number of counting books and rhymes. When children are reading counting books, we have an ideal opportunity to make the counting process explicit and to teach important skills. These books come in many shapes and sizes, and every Early Years setting should have a selection which will appeal to children's different interests.

Look for counting books where objects are randomly scattered on the page: the challenge for the children is how to keep track of what has been counted while still focussing on the counting sequence.

You will want to encourage children to share reading counting books and rhymes together. Looking at how counting can be used in different situations and with different materials can lead to high levels of mathematical discussion. Talk about techniques of counting and problems that might need to be solved when you are counting. You could model some solutions: for example, show how to move things that need to be counted into a straight line to make counting easier.

Counting books are complemented by the inclusion of number rhymes in the routine of every day to help children with early literacy and numeracy. Focus children's attention and give experience of data collection by organising a vote for a number rhyme. Make a list of three rhymes and give each child a voting counter. Ask them to put it on the copy of the rhyme or book they liked best. Together, count the number of votes. Try to include favourite traditional and contemporary rhymes as well as rhymes that children bring from home to nursery. Support children by giving enough rehearsal time and space to use their new-found mathematical words and ideas about counting.

Introducing number rhymes

Every week, choose a rhyme together with the children and sing it at group times to give the children the opportunity to learn or revisit the words. Wherever possible, choose rhymes with actions as these will help the children remember the rhymes.

Use musical instruments to accompany the singing. Count in to start: "One, two, three ... This time, I'm going to count to 5 before we start singing." Develop children's sense of the rhythmic quality of counting by playing clapping games such as 'Touch your knee and clap'. When all the children are involved, increase the clapping to touch, clap, clap, clap and count the claps aloud. Involve the children by inviting them to suggest the pattern of counting and touching. These invented action games with their fun repetition are a great way for children to learn the order of the numbers.

Make a recording of the rhymes with the children, so that families have easy access to the words and, where appropriate, tunes. In this way, families and practitioners can work together to support children's early learning through familiar rhymes.

Play 'Musical count to 5' with 10 beanbags numbered 1 to 5. Play some music while the group pass the beanbags round the circle. When the music stops, the children throw the appropriately numbered beanbag that they are holding into the centre of the circle as you read a number rhyme aloud.

Supporting counting and number rhymes

Develop children's mathematical understanding through rhymes and songs and linked imaginative play.

Children should have access to props which help them retell number rhymes, in a similar way that they are used to support the retelling of stories. Provide a selection of materials so that children can use different media to illustrate one of the numbers and put the pages together to make a big counting book.

You can buy sets of five 'little ducks' or 'speckled frogs' and puppets. However, it is much more fun to include children and their families in making collections to support counting rhymes. Encourage everyone to track down frogs, elephants, aliens or monsters and other paraphernalia (it doesn't matter whether the objects are big, small, plastic, rubber or furry) and use any five (or 10) to support the rhymes.

It doesn't matter if one of the sets gets damaged, dirty or lost, as another one can be added so easily. Of course, there may not be too many 'currant buns' which aren't edible in many homes, so it is also worth considering planning to make some cakes, buns and jam tarts from salt dough to use to support both role play and the retelling of the rhyme.

After a successful session of number songs, you could take the group for a maths walk so that children could look for the numbers that they have been singing about. The best maths walks give time to look at and photograph things at children's eye level. Provide bags to make collections of objects. Later, look through photos together and encourage children to reflect and talk about what they remember from the walk and examine the found objects. Make a 3D model of your walking route and mark where you can find numbers.

Making salt dough numbers

Ingredients:

2 cups plain flour

1 cup salt

1 cup water

1 tablespoon lemon juice

1 tablespoon vegetable oil

What to do:

Ask the children to mix the ingredients and knead until pliable. Get them to roll out the dough and cut out numbers. Bake them for at least three hours in a very slow oven at 100 °C (200 °F/Gas Mark 1/4). When they are fully dried out on both sides, turn off the oven and allow to cool.

Children can then paint and decorate the salt dough numbers in any way they wish. Finally, seal the rock-hard shapes with PVA glue, allow to dry and suspend with ribbon from a decorative branch to make a number tree.

Most children will be able to recognise some number symbols long before they are able to write them, especially numerals which are important to them. Encourage them to use number names to five and, later, to 10. It is helpful if we occasionally model some maths by writing numbers and also build in opportunities for children to make their own maths writing.

Ask the group to sit in a circle and roll a large ball to someone sitting opposite who then rolls the ball to someone else sitting in the circle, with everyone counting the rolls. Draw children's attention to one of your counting books to support their counting. You could decide in advance how many ball rolls you are going to do: "Let's roll the ball round the circle five times, so let's find that number in the book."

Use number cards to record how many ball rolls were made.

Five Fat Teddies sitting on a wall
(to the tune of 'Ten green bottles')

Five fat teddies sitting on the wall

Five fat teddies sitting on the wall

And if one fat teddy should accidentally fall

Ahhhh!

There would be four fat teddies sitting on the wall.

Four fat teddies …

Three fat teddies …

Two fat teddies …

One fat teddy sitting on the wall

One fat teddy sitting on the wall

And if that fat teddy should accidentally fall

Ahhhh!

There would be NO fat teddies sitting on the wall.

You will need:

- A cardboard box decorated to look like a wall

- Five assorted teddies

What to do:

❈ Chant or sing the rhyme with the children, pushing one bear off the wall each time as the rhyme continues.

❈ Ask the children to predict how many bears will be left and count together to confirm.

❈ Encourage the children to take the lead, helping the bears fall off the wall independently.

Questions to support mathematical thinking and problem solving:

Can you guess how many teddies there are altogether?

Can you tell me how many there will be if one falls down?

What can we do to check?

What would happen if two teddies fell off instead of one?

Maths learning

Enjoy joining in with number songs and rhymes

Count up to five objects by saying one number name for each item

Say with confidence the number that is one less than a given number

Find one less than a number to five

Vocabulary

one less, less than, one, two, three, four, five, how many?, count, count back, rhyme, number

Extensions:

◆ Encourage the children to act as 'teddies', retelling the rhymes and falling off the wall. Make headbands that the children can wear when acting out rhymes. Laminate strips of coloured card and attach long strips of Velcro to each end of the cards (so that they will fit different sizes of head) and a piece of Velcro to the front (so that the children can attach the 'bear' props to them). The headbands can be used with other props such as frogs, ducks, aliens or buns.

◆ Make up different versions of the rhyme with the children – kind children, small kittens – and make books to match.

Ten in a Bed

Ten in a Bed by Penny Dale (Walker, 1990) was the first in the series of books, involving the same characters (*Ten out of Bed* is another delightful example). The great thing about this book is that it can be so easily adapted to include any 10 soft toys which the children select. All it needs is a bit of imagination and enthusiasm!

Making 'Ten in a Bed' books and number lines

Maths learning

Respond orally to simple addition questions

Tell own addition stories

Count on one from any number between 1 and 9

Vocabulary

one more, how many?, add on, total, count

You will need:

• A cardboard or wooden bed
• Ten soft toys and puppets in a wicker basket
• A digital camera

What to do:

✳ Support the children as they take turns to choose a toy from the basket and put it in the bed.

✳ Support the children to take a digital image of the toy in the bed.

✳ Keep adding the toys, one at a time, taking a new image every time.

✳ Encourage the children to predict how many toys there will be when one more is added and count together to confirm.

✳ Continue until there are 10 soft toys in the bed.

✳ With the children, print out the images and create an 'adding' number book with the numerals on each page.

Questions to support mathematical thinking and problem solving;

Can you tell me why you chose that toy?

Can you explain why you think the elephant won't fit in the bed?

Can you tell us what is similar about those two toys? What is different?

What will we need to make a number book about the toys?

What can we say about the toys in the bed?

What would happen if we took two toys out of the bed at the same time?

Other related activities:

◆ Plan a 'Ten in a Bed' session outdoors, with 10 children taking turns to 'fall out' of a large blanket.

◆ Put all 10 toys next to the bed, remove a certain number when the children aren't looking, put them in the bed and cover them up with a 'quilt'. Count the number of toys 'out of bed' and ask children to predict how many are in the bed. Count together to check.

◆ Make a 'Ten in a Bed' game, with a dice with just one dot on three faces, two dots on one face and no dots on two faces. Children start off with 10 small soft toys or pictures of 10 toys each in a cardboard box bed. They take turns to roll the dice and remove the correct number of toys. The child with the first empty bed is the winner.

Extensions:

◆ Extend the activity, taking out one toy each time and taking another image. Make a second book with 'one less' on each page.

◆ Look at the two counting books together and notice the similarities and differences.

◆ Print out a second set of images, fix each to an A4 card, laminate and use to form a number line for the home corner, number reference area or outdoors.

◆ Use the images to create matching games or to play pelmanism (Kim's game, see p21).

Books about number rhymes:

Title	Author	Publisher
Ten Little Speckled Frogs	Jess Stockholm	Child's Play, 2003
Ten Fat Sausages	Tina Foreman	Child's Play, 2001
Ten Little Monkeys	Tina Foreman	Child's Play, 2001
Ten Little Babies	Lisa Kopper	Frances Lincoln, 2000
Five Little Men in a Flying Saucer	Dan Crisp	Child's Play, 2005
Five Little Ducks	Ian Beck	Orchard, 1999
Ten Green Bottles	Audrey Thomas	Bright Sparks, 2000

Collections of rhymes:

Title	Author	Publisher
Ten in the Bed and Other Number Rhymes	Zita Newcombe	Walker, 2004
Number Rhymes to Say and Play	Opal Dunn	Frances Lincoln, 2005
Ten Little Fingers – 100 Number Rhymes for Children	Louise Binder	LDA, 2000
Fun with Number Rhymes for the Early Years	Julie Hodgson	Brilliant, 2005
Counting Rhymes	John Foster	OUP, 1998

Chapter 6

From traditional tales to a fantasy world

Oh, and the tiniest Billy Goat Gruff went up the hillside where he met the huge dinosaurs. But they were all very friendly and played games.

Matthew, 5, in a group discussion

The enjoyment that comes from listening to stories and 'reading' books is motivational in itself for young children, and traditional tales provide a good context for mathematical exploration. Children will come to Early Years settings with experiences of hearing traditional stories read or told by family members or from watching animated versions on video or television. If we look at them closely, traditional tales are set in a make-believe fantasy world already, and fantasy can sometimes come from a traditional tale as a modern story quite naturally while children are engaged in free play and transgress the boundaries set by the tale.

Build on all children's home experiences by providing well-illustrated traditional tales which are familiar and introducing those which are less well known. Looking at the illustrations together and exploring the maths elements in them will lead to fruitful mathematical discussions. Questions starting with "I wonder what" or "Where do you think …?" that give potential for suppositions such as "What do you suppose is behind/above/next to the little fox?" will enrich any maths conversation, as will questions such as "I can't see where the spotty dog is on the page. Can you?" that invite participants to put forward their ideas in the spirit of developing a learning community – especially so if we model or invite another child to provide the commentary and description of where another member of the group is pointing.

After a more structured, guided approach, give children plenty of time to re-enact what they have learned in free play where their imagination can take them into the wild and wonderful realms of fantasy.

Many traditional tales include specific numbers of characters or objects:

* *Goldilocks and the Three Bears*
* *The Three Little Pigs*
* *Snow White and the Seven Dwarves*
* *The Wolf and the Seven Little Kids*
* *Udea and her Seven Brothers*

Other stories encourage an exploration of size:

* *The Great Big Enormous Turnip*
* *Jack and the Beanstalk*
* *The Elves and the Shoe Maker*
* *Cinderella*

Trails and journeys also feature strongly in many traditional tales:

* *The Gingerbread Man*
* *Hansel and Gretel*
* *Chicken Licken*
* *Sindbad the Sailor*

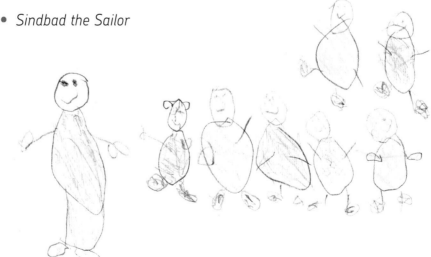

The Elves and the Shoemaker

This magical 19th-century tale by the Brothers Grimm is about dreams coming true, perfect for explaining the basics of doubling of simple numbers. You can demonstrate what happens when you begin a doubling sequence by using collections of different objects. Children will understand that, in the shoemaker's case, this makes for a vast amount of pairs of shoes within a short time, so no wonder that the shoemaker becomes wealthy so quickly!

Sorting shoes

You will need:

- Different-sized shoe boxes
- Assorted shoes and boots

What to do:

❈ Encourage the children to explore the footwear, sorting them, using own criteria, or finding pairs.

❈ Support them as they predict which shoes will fit into which boxes.

Questions to support mathematical thinking and problem solving:

What can we do to remind us which shoes fit in each box?

Can you guess how many shoes and boots there are all together?

How do you think we could find the best pair of shoes for the doll?

Can you explain why you think those two make a good pair?

Why do you think that is the best box for those boots?

Can you tell us what is similar about those two shoes?
What is different?

Maths learning
Use language such as 'smaller' and 'bigger'
Order two items by length
Use size language such as 'big', 'small', or 'little'

Vocabulary
big, large, small, little, bigger than, smaller than, size

Stone Soup

Stone Soup is a less well-known traditional tale based on a familiar and recurring theme: the sly old fox. The gist of the story is that Mr Fox is very hungry, and he really would like a bowl of soup, but he doesn't have any food or any money. All he has is a big pot, a spoon and a stone. So he travels to all the animals in the forest, shows them his pot of 'soup', stirs it around and says: "Mmh, wonderful soup, all it needs now is a carrot." This goes on until he has collected lots of vegetables. Then, of course, he really can make a pot of delicious soup!

Making soup

You will need:

- A pot or saucepan
- A large wooden spoon
- A variety of vegetables

What to do:

✳ Retell the story with the children, acting out the parts of different animals, holding on vegetable in each hand.

✳ 'Mr Fox' goes to each animal in turn, asking for one or two vegetables. Each child has to choose whether to give one or two vegetables, then everyone predicts how many will be in the pot: "If we have four vegetables already and we add one more, how many will we have?"

Questions to support mathematical thinking and problem solving:

Can you guess how many vegetables are in the pot?

How many vegetables do you think can fit into the pot?

What can we do to check how many will fit?

Extensions:

◆ Making vegetable soup with real vegetables, using a balance, cutting different-sized pieces, sharing out the vegetables fairly

◆ Writing and illustrating a vegetable soup recipe

◆ Creating repeating patterns, using vegetable printing

Maths learning

Count reliably to 10 objects

Use number names in familiar contexts

Begin to use vocabulary involved in addition in practical activities

Find one more than a number from 1 to 10

Vocabulary

how many?, add, more, enough, too few, too many, less than, more than

---

The Three Billy Goats Gruff

The Three Billy Goats Gruff is one of several traditional tales which enables children to explore the 'threeness of three' and consider size in a meaningful way. It has the added advantage of a 'monster', in this case a troll, which hides under a bridge rather than a bed!

You will need:

- Three goats in different sizes (from a pack of farm animals)
- A troll-like creature
- A bridge
- Shiny blue paper, blue chiffon or real water
- Real or fake grass
- A black tray

What to do:

- Ensure the children are familiar with the story.
- Set up an imaginative play scenario, with the troll under the bridge over the water and the three goats on one side of the river.
- Write '1st', '2nd' and '3rd' and '1', '2' and '3' on laminated cards.
- Support the children as they retell the story, emphasising the order in which they try to cross the bridge and the size of the goats.

Questions to support mathematical thinking and problem solving:

Can you tell me which Billy goat tries to cross the bridge first?

How do you think we could help the goats get past the troll?

Can you tell us what is similar about the goats? What is different?

Extensions:

- Provide the same scenario, with no bridge but with a variety of different construction resources. Support children as they use 3D materials to construct their own bridge.
- Recreate the scene outdoors, with a chalked river and a 'bridge' made from an overturned wooden seesaw or large wooden blocks. Encourage the children to act out the story.

Maths learning

Count to three objects by saying one number name for each

Know that the last number said is the number of objects in the group

Order three items by size

Vocabulary

small, smaller, smallest, big, bigger, biggest, first, second, third, one, two, three, under, over

Making the most of dinosaurs

It is important to find tales and storybooks which appeal to children who are not naturally drawn to stories. This group includes a high proportion of boys, who may be more interested in informative texts and some who enjoy active, physical play and like to be outdoors. Their interest may include dinosaurs, monsters and wheeled toys. Capitalise on these interests and focus on key elements. One of the fascinations of dinosaurs is their sheer size. Wherever possible, plan a trip to a museum where children can stand frozen in awe at the sheer hugeness of dinosaur bones.

Harry and the Bucket Full of Dinosaurs

A lovely book for inspiration and to work with is Ian Whybrow's *Harry and the Bucket Full of Dinosaurs* (Puffin, 2003). Five-year-old Harry has a bucket full of dinosaurs who talk to him, but seem to be toys to the other characters in the book.

Maths learning

Use mathematical descriptive and comparative language

Begin to use the appropriate vocabulary of measures

Begin to use non-standard measures

Use two non-standard measures to make comparisons

Vocabulary

describe, measure, big, huge, enormous, vast, great, large, gigantic, massive, great, mammoth, titanic, colossal, gargantuan, immense, cosmic, outsized, hefty, monumental

The 'Big words' game

You will need:

- An outline or a large-scale painting of a dinosaur, preferably covering one wall or at least a large display board
- Dinosaur-shaped paper footprints and fat markers

What to do:

❋ Talk to the children about words you can use to describe size. Ask them for suggestions for similar words to describe dinosaurs. Encourage the children to go home and speak to family members and come back the next day with suggestions such as: *huge, enormous, vast, great, large, gigantic, massive, great, mammoth, titanic, colossal, gargantuan, immense, cosmic, outsized, hefty, monumental.* Support the children as they make up their own descriptive words to describe such huge creatures.

❋ Act as a scribe to write the children's suggestions onto the footprints and stick these onto the display. Encourage the children to use the descriptive words in everyday conversation.

✳ Use a reference book with the children to look up the size of a dinosaur and chalk out the size in the outdoor area.

✳ Use common everyday objects as a snon-standard unit to measure the length and height of the dinosaur. Estimate how many children long the dinosaur is, then measure.

Questions to support mathematical thinking and problem solving:

Can you guess how many children tall the dinosaur is?

What can we do to find out?

What can we say about the size of the dinosaurs?

If the dinosaur came to visit us, would it fit through the door?

Moving like dinosaurs

Apart from the mathematical aspects, a lively game such as this encourages children to be physically active and energetic and provides an opportunity for them to use the language of movement.

You will need:

• Computer-generated pictures of dinosaurs

What to do:

✳ Discuss the dinosaur pictures with the children and talk about the ways in which they may move.

✳ Spend time exploring different ways of moving.

✳ Play 'follow the leader', moving in different ways and creating different repeating patterns with movement.

Maths learning

Repeat, continue or create a pattern of movements

Use the language of size

Vocabulary

stride, step, big, huge, tiny, one, two, three, hop

Questions to support mathematical thinking and problem solving:

How do you think we could describe the dinosaur's steps?

Why do you think a diplodocus takes bigger steps than a Tyrannosaurus rex?

Can you think of a way to move like a brontosaurus?

What can we say about the ways we are moving?

A good idea

Dinosaurs lend themselves to a display on a large scale. After exploring picture books about the creatures, encourage children to draw their own pictures of dinosaurs. Photocopy these onto overhead acetates (alternatively, scan them into a PC and create a Powerpoint presentation). Finally, use an overhead or data projector to project the images onto a blank wall. Children can compare the small versions of their drawings with the huge images on the wall. When they have had lots of time to investigate the images, cover the wall with lining paper and choose one or two to copy onto the wall, using large decorators' brushes and thick paint. These images can then be used as the basis for a display or a dinosaur museum role-play area.

Other books with a dinosaur theme:

Title	Author	Publisher
Dinosaur Roar!	Henrietta Strickland	Koala Books, 2005
Dinosaurs Galore!	Giles Andreae	Tiger Tales, 2006
Stomp, Chomp, Big Roars! Here Come the Dinosaurs	Kaye Umansky	Penguin Books, 2006
The Dance of the Dinosaurs	Colin Hawkins	Collins Picture Books, 2003
Saturday Night at the Dinosaur Stomp	Carol Diggory Shields	Candlewick Press, 1997

Giants, castles, treasure and all that!

Jack and the Beanstalk

Jack and the Beanstalk is a perennial favourite with children and adults alike, and there are several themes running through it. The idea of a giant offers opportunities to explore size, and fantasy stories that include castles, palaces and forests suggest maps and routes and large constructions. Magic beans, of course, often lead to the ultimate prize – gold or other treasure.

Magic beans

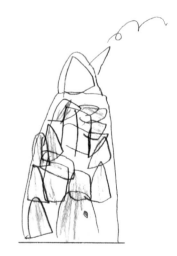

Magic beans are easy to make: outdoors or in a well-ventilated room (away from children) spread a bag of dried butter beans over several layers of newspaper, ensuring one side of the beans are facing upwards. Spray the beans with non-toxic metallic paint – silver or gold looks great. Once the magic beans are dry, they can be used in many ways.

You will need:

- Magic beans
- Small shiny boxes in different shapes or sizes
- Sticky notes and metallic markers

What to do:

❈ Support the children as they explore the beans, counting them and filling and emptying the boxes.

❈ Encourage the children to record how many beans are in the boxes.

❈ Play 'More or less?'. Count the number of beans in a box with one child. Ask the other children in the group to guess how many beans are in the box. If someone says '10' and there are '15', say 'more'; if someone says '20', say 'less' until the children have guessed the correct number.

Questions to support mathematical thinking and problem solving:

Can you guess how many beans are in the biggest box if there are 10 beans in the smallest box?

Can you think of a number that is more than 7 and less than 10?

Maths learning

Use pictures, symbols and numerals to record numbers

Estimate the number of objects in a group with a reasonable prediction and then count to confirm

Find the number one more or one less than a number from 1 to 20

Vocabulary

more than, less than, how many?, number, numeral, record

How do you think we could remember the number of beans in the box?

Can you explain why you think the number could be 8 or 9?

Why do you think there are more beans in that box?

What was the first thing you did when you were counting the beans?

Extensions:

◆ Magic beans can be used as an alternative to dice in board games. Count out six beans with the children and roll them from a small container. Count together how many land, gold side up. Move that many places.

◆ Use 10 magic beans to explore number bonds to 10: "If three land gold side up, how many are white side up? What if there are four, gold side up?"

◆ Estimate how many beans can be grabbed with one hand. Count and check. Try the other hand.

◆ Try laying beans on a flat tray and moving them, one at a time, with chopsticks, tweezers or tongs. How many can be moved before a tocker or sand timer runs out?

Treasure chest

You will need:

- Large treasure box and treasure
- Four small treasure boxes (for example, jewellery boxes) or gold plates
- A dice

What to do:

✳ Support the children as they take turns to choose 10 items from the box, choosing just one at a time and explaining their choice.

✳ When every child has 10 items, they take turns to roll the dice and give that number of items to the child on their left.

✳ The child who gives all their treasure away first is the winner.

Questions to support mathematical thinking and problem solving:

Can you tell me why you chose that first?

Why do you think that you need 3 more to make 10 if you have 8 already?

Can you think of a way to make that fair?

What did you notice about the gold coins?

Can you tell us what is similar about the necklaces? What is different?

What can we say about the treasure in your box?

Maths learning

Count to 10 everyday objects by saying one number name for each item

Respond orally to simple addition and subtracting questions

Understand the meaning of 'more' and 'less'

Vocabulary

more than, less than, count, add, take away, subtract

Treasure

No Early Years setting would be complete without a 'treasure chest' full to the brim with booty. This could be an old jewellery box, a gold-covered, sequined cardboard box with a lid or a chest found at a car-boot sale. It should be filled with 'precious things' which could include nuggets and gems from educational suppliers, junk jewellery rings, earrings, necklaces, watches, foreign coins, beads, buttons, shells, Christmas tree decorations or shiny cracker gifts. Wherever possible, ask family and community members to contribute unwanted 'loot'.

Introduce treasure to children, using the following activities:

* Panning for gold and gems with sieves and colanders in water
* Fishing for treasure in water or while using magnetic fishing games
* Using metal detectors outdoors or in sand or potting compost indoors
* Digging for 'buried treasure' outdoors or indoors
* Using sieves or tongs with dry sand and glitter
* Using treasure as part of small-world play for pirates or retelling favourite pirates tales

Books featuring traditional tales:

Title	Author	Publisher
Goldilocks and the Three Bears	Penelope Lively	Hodder, 2004
The Three Little Pigs	Richard Johnson	Child's Play, 2004
The Three Billy Goats Gruff	Nick Sharratt	MacMillan, 2004
Hansel and Gretel	Andea Petrlik	Child's Play, 2005
Jack and the Beanstalk	Richard Walker	Barefoot Books, 2006
The True Story of Chicken Licken	Jan Omerod	Walker, 1999
Babouska	Arthur Scholey	Lion Hudson, 2002
Mariana and the Merchild	Caroline Pitcher	Frances Lincoln, 2007
Rainbow Bird	Eric Maddern	Frances Lincoln, 1996
The True Story of the Three Little Pigs	John Scieszka	Puffin, 1991
Mixed Up Fairy Tales	Hilary Robinson	Hodder, 2005
The Wolf's Story – What Really Happened to Little Red Riding Hood	Toby Forward	Walker, 2005
Fairytale News	Colin Hawkins	Walker, 2005
Aesop's Funky Fairy Tales	Vivian French	Puffin, 1999
Jim and the Beanstalk	Raymond Briggs	Putman, 1997
Little Red Hen	Jonathan Allen	Corgi, 2003
Jasper's Beanstalk	Nick Butterworth	Hodder, 2006
Almost Traditional Tales	Ros Bayley	Laurence Educational, 2006
The Three Little Wolves and the Big Bad Pig	Eugenios Trivizas	Prentice Hall, 1993
Once Upon a Time	John Prater	Walker, 2005
Just a Friendly Old Troll	Alvin Granowsky	Steck-Vaughn, 1996
Beware of Boys	Tony Blundell	Puffin, 2003
Beware of Girls	Tony Blundell	Puffin, 2002

Chapter 7

Planning for maths from stories

Good planning is the key to making children's maths learning effective, exciting, varied and progressive.

Planning for learning in the Foundation Stage

Traditional and contemporary books and stories, poems and rhymes are an exciting and stimulating resource we can use in our planning to build on what children already know. The strength of using stories as one of our resource vehicles is that stories and books come in all shapes and sizes and we know that there will be a book that is just right for a particular child at a particular time. We can therefore plan not only relevant learning experiences but challenging learning experiences, tailored to children's individual needs and stages of development.

Research such as the EPPE has shown that freely chosen play activities provide the best opportunities for practitioners to extend children's thinking. We need to plan how, and where, we can create opportunities to extend child-initiated play as well as adult-directed group work, using a story as a starter or as a support for further experiences.

We can feel reassured that it really doesn't matter what an Early Years curriculum is called: it is the principles that underpin it that matter, and a curriculum that promotes an approach led by continuous, observational assessment will be successful. Making time to talk to parents and carers about their children's interests, together with an ongoing observational assessment, will provide you with an insightful knowledge of each child's achievements. This, in turn, will enable you to identify children's learning priorities and inform your planning for a range of play-based, multisensory learning experiences across the setting.

Medium-term maths planner

Number
*Count reliably
to 10 objects*

Recognise numerals

Play experiences
Small world – jungle tray

Role play – jungle animal
house

Planned activities
Jungle animals number line

Outdoors – jungle animals
number track
game

Calculation
*Use the vocabulary of
adding and subtracting*

Find one more and one less

Play experiences
Jungle animals picnic party

Book area – listening to
animal nursery
rhyme tape
(and one more)

Planned activities
Drama - act out story,
using puppets

Dice game with characters

Monkey Puzzle
by Julia Donaldson and Axel Schleffer

Shape and space
Recognise patterns

*Describe shapes and
position*

Play experiences
Outdoors - animal hide-
and-seek

Construction – building
animal houses

Planned activities
Art workshop – butterfly
painting

Creative area - string
spider webs

Measures
*Use language such as
'shorter' or 'longer'
to describe length*

*Use everyday words
to describe position*

Play experiences
Playing with caterpillar
sticks

Role play – shop selling
jungle survival
equipment

Planned activities
Animal descriptions

Feely-bag animals

Using and applying
*Match sets of animals
to a numeral*

*Use maths ideas to solve
a practical problem*

Play experiences
Outdoors – jungle trail

Outdoors - where is
the monkey?

Planned activities
Animal-matching game

Jungle-wall collage

Effective planning starts with observing the children with a view to identifying their particular interests and learning needs and then, together with colleagues, planning the next step in the children's learning journeys. Most planning formats have a three-stage structure: a long-term plan which covers mostly an academic year, a medium-term plan which usually covers between two and six weeks and a short-term plan which, in general, demonstrates what will happen over daily or weekly periods. Any short-term plan can only be an indicator, as it will need to be flexible enough to be tailored for individual children's learning and development needs.

What you will see illustrated are two plans: a medium-term plan, where a book is the focus, and a short-term plan – a small-group daily plan.

Our aim will always be for children to become confident users of mathematical ideas who can articulate their understanding and demonstrate and discuss their ideas, who talk about maths, who draw, write, use symbols, who simply enjoy maths. Using books, stories and rhymes is one way for children to learn to do just that.

Short-term plan	Wednesday morning session – small group
Context book:	*Kipper's Birthday*
Workshop area:	Indoors, malleable
Area of learning and development:	Problem solving, reasoning and numeracy
Learning intention:	To count up to five/10 objects accurately (Extension: To say how many more are needed to make a given number)
Opportunities for assessment:	Do children count accurately to five (10)? Do they know that the last number said tells us how many there are? Do they understand that the number of cakes/cases/candles is not affected by their position? Do they respond to simple addition/subtraction questions?
Targeted children:	Children who are using number names in the correct order to 5+, but do not use one-to-one correspondence consistently (Children who are counting to 10 accurately and are beginning to add/subtract)
Experience/Activity:	Rolling out dough, cutting cakes, placing cake cases and cakes in trays, counting cases, cakes and candles/holders
Resources:	Rolling pins, cooked play dough, cutters, 6- and 12-hole cake-baking trays, cake cases, birthday candles and holders, paper plates
Adult input and questions:	I wonder how many cakes can we fit in this tray? Does it help if you point as you count? Does it help if you put them in the tray first? How can we find out how many full cases there are altogether? If we need six all together and you have four, how many more do we need?